BIRTHMARKS and BRUISES

A Collection of poems and photographs

on various emotions and feelings.

VOLUME 1

DR ROB RAFEEK HENRY

Archway Publishing books may be ordered through booksellers or by contacting:

Archway Publishing
1663 Liberty Drive
Bloomington, IN 47403
www.archwaypublishing.com
844-669-3957

ISBN: 978-1-6657-1512-6 (sc)
ISBN: 978-1-6657-1513-3 (hc)
ISBN: 978-1-6657-1511-9 (e)

Print information available on the last page.

Archway Publishing rev. date: 12/01/2021

CONTENTS

INTRODUCTION

Emotions can be interpreted differently based on various life experiences; they are entirely subjective. This collection of poems describes an incomplete list of emotions and feelings. Written in my final year of dental school in the suburbs of Chicago, many of these emotions were constantly expressed and witnessed by myself and everyone who surrounded me, including my family, friends, patients, faculty, and staff. Poetry is an art that allows the mind to wonder, the heart to jump, and the soul to dance. I hope you enjoy reading them as much as I enjoyed feeling and writing them.

My primary intention for publishing this collection of poems is to reach within myself and extract the deeper, internalized, intangible feelings of each of these moments. To allow myself to surrender to each of these feelings and truly describe them on paper and in photos. Equally as important is to admit to myself that I am capable of feeling and releasing these emotions into the world. Each poem is accompanied by photos, captured by me, to depict the exact feeling in that moment. Though I understand it's difficult to demand emotions upon immediate request, with limited time and resources, my willing volunteers did an excellent job. (mostly colleagues from dental school)

My second intention for publishing this collection is to allow others to feel connected. We are becoming more and more divided as a world, whether through economic status, political views, educational limitations, or cultural variations. However, there is no question that feelings like love, pain, and joy are witnessed by every single living being. Emotional intelligence, as with everything in life, requires a fine balance. I hope that you spread joy when capable, and recharge when needed. But mostly that you understand that in this big world of ours, you are never alone.

My third goal for publishing these poems is to allow for another form of entertainment and self-reflection. Sit with your coffee, tea, chocolate milk, water, wine, beer, even a stiff drink, and read one poem. Look at the photos associated with them. Reflect on the words, look at the photos you are drawn more to, and think about what that person was feeling in the moment the image was captured. Then sit back and think about what that specific emotion means to you. When was the last time you felt that way? When was the last time you saw this emotion on your partner's face, your friend's face? Think about how these emotions control the path in your life. List its priority in your life or on the scale that it guides your path. Ask yourself what you can do to feel more of it, less of it, or question its presence at all. Breathe and look at another poem.

My fourth goal is for this piece to end up on your coffee table. The next time you and your friends, your children, your nieces, nephews, or grandchildren are visiting, open it to any poem. Read the poem aloud, or don't. Skip to the photos, sit for a minute in silence to gather your thoughts, and then discuss that emotion. Listen to what your grandchildren think about hope or excitement or anxiety or love. Listen to what your grandparents think about happiness, fear, or loneliness.

My final goal for publishing this collection is to be able to donate to charitable causes, whether through scholarships in poetry, dentistry, or other forms of art, or through direct help to other less-fortunate individuals in immediate need.

Allow my interpretations of each of these emotions and feelings into your heart, mind, and soul.

WORDS

Words are powerful.

Words are the heaviest and simplest of tools ever known.
Words can be sharp and pierce through flesh quicker than any blade—
"You're fat!"
Words can be blunt and dull and gnaw away at souls better than any parasite—
"You're too skinny!"
But words can be juicy and sweet and change the course of any conversation—
"You're voluptuous!"

Words can follow rules, or better, words can be rearranged to break standards.
Words can be simple, fun, sometimes confusing.
Words can have one meaning, two meanings, many, many more.
More important, words are fibers strung together to display the tapestry of your inner core.

Words have been used to start wars, end them.
Used carelessly, words can break hearts, shed tears, and destroy families, friendships, lives.
Words are powerful!
But words can initiate change and birth new feelings of hope and positivity, happiness.
Here are some of my words, assembled as poems.

ANGER

The most irrational of your brothers, you are unpredictable;
Your range in volume settles between plotting silence and bellowing rage.
You lack all beauty, your teeth fully exposed, lines covering your face.
Your scent is immense and warning, like spoiled milk.
You are vastly unnecessary.

You are overused, personality never amused.
Your hands break bones and leave marks.
Your voice shatters hearts and hopes alike.
Your disdain grows solely from within.
You are vastly unnecessary.

Your presence is abused, always leaving a bitter taste.
A turn of the head and a deep breath avoids your destruction.
Inner calm stifles your wrath; rationality grounds your itching feet.
Your punches always precede regret.
You are vastly unnecessary.
…or are you?

ANXIETY

It sneaks up on you, agitated and all-encompassing.
You are exhausted, but your eyes are widened, your muscles taut.
Heartbeats compete with the nerves in your shaking limbs to cross the nonexistent finish line.
The tightening of your chest, the shortened breath, the familiarity of "Why now?"
The panic as it engulfs you—all of you.

Hours, days, maybe years of shaken legs and worn teeth from bitten pencils,
The bellyaches of unknown causes, and the large gulps that follow those.
The gnawing of lips and nails and chips and angst.
The nausea of a large swallowed pill, absent water.
Confusion and questions gush in, mostly at bedtime.

Measured in tons of tears, gallons of vomit, and hours of wasted, restless sleep.
You drink to drown out the doubt or to purposely delay clarity.
You are still; you are almost at the end of this episode—almost—
Until the momentum of the bouncing ball revs up, and the couch begs for you to curl up.
You anxiously await the next inevitable episode.

A PATHETIC

Sometimes it's the constant rejection;
Other times it's simply another morning.
Apathy looks at you, robe wrinkled, decaffeinated coffee in hand,
No care, no thoughts, no urgency—just there.

Sometimes it's because your voice is unheard;
Other times it's because the wrong ears are present.
Apathy tastes like the same old turkey sandwich, bland and dry.
You chew the last bite, waiting for your soapbox or maybe someone new to touch.

Sometimes it's because you know there are bigger things to care about;
Other times it's because you don't want to be misunderstood, to be right.
Apathy sounds like the perfectly monotone electrical buzzing of the wall outlet,
A subtle reminder to its presence—quickly ignored and forgotten. Meh.

Sometimes it's because you've seen the worst in others;
Other times it's because you're scared to find the truth about yourself.
Apathy feels like the flat-chested, overly shrugged shoulders of mediocrity.
Easily confused with purposeful silence, apathy is indifferent to this moment—and most.

BEAUTY

Beauty is the nerve bundles that ignite your heart,
Hearts that beat faster at the sight of men, women, both.
Beauty is the elastic fibers that make your skin one,
Skin that stretches to house fetus, fat, marks.
Beauty is the rich hemoglobin-filled blood vessels,
Vessels that make you feel in heat, cold, numbness.

Beauty is within you.

Beauty is the light that shines on others on your hard days,
Brighter on days when you feel dark, broken, invisible.
Beauty is the care for the preciousness of life,
Caring harder for people more helpless, hurt, forgotten.
Beauty is the celebration of other cultures with pride,
Cheering harder in the presence of oppression, shame, war.

Beauty is within you.

Beauty is the desire of a broader mind's view, visionary,
A view that inspires you to scrape into art, philosophy, physics.
Beauty is the altruistic goal of sharing love,
Love that aims to the shallowest, hardened, burnt.
Beauty is the hope of peace, breathing, stillness,
Mostly subjective, often unseen, unheard.

Beauty is within you.

CONTENT

A rare being you are, most transient, briefly devoured.
You feel like check marks meeting eager boxes.
Like overdue, ignored bills finally paid, shredded.
Anxiety rid, exam passed, team made kind of grunts.
A rare being you are, most transient, briefly devoured.

A rare being you are, most transient, briefly devoured.
Rarely too savory or toothachingly sweet, never bitter.
Your dough fills to satisfaction, gluttony unseen.
Lungs exhale retained breaths from anguished days, weeks, months.
A rare being you are, most transient, briefly devoured.

A rare being you are, most transient, briefly devoured.
The stage after the pimple has popped but before the redness ensues.
The removed weight on my back, the load finally lightened.
The nights of silence, the nights of hope, nights of inner calm.
A rare being you are, most transient, briefly devoured.

COURAGE

When the path is dark, undiscovered, feared,
Your reassuring eyes shine the cobblestone steps.
When verbal darts pierce my soul, crush me,
Your centered affirmation clears my mind.

When fear limits my creativity, intentions,
Your strong will guides my pen filled with ink.
When blatant injustices are painted over, purposely ignored,
Your unrelenting reminders widen my tunnel vision.

When it's easier to feel nothing, ruffle no feathers,
Your rosy lips flutter my passive heart, sound alarms.
When all hope is lost,
Your waving hands shake my being,
A reminder to stand firm, head raised high.

CURIOSITY

You smell like something fattening, and your smile is incomplete.
Your eye color a mysterious hazel-brown, lids always squinted.
You feel like comfort and questionable tight leather.
But your taste never quenches my pondering thirst.

Your powers transcend toddlers and puppies and aged men.
Your disbursement can be fruitful or poisonous.
Your label has bolded warnings, the bottle never empty, never filled.
The gamble of knowing cannot be undone.

Though you may have killed the cat,
Your beauty showers the pet graveyard in bright dandelions.
You are a prerequisite to innovation, creativity and puzzling dreams.
You are risky; you are necessary; you are mostly worth it.

DEPRESSED

The baby silenced, ashes blown, sun dimmed.
Commence the maze of darkness.
The tart berries and sweet honey slip away.
Tongue tied, heart twisted, faces battered.
Cries are no longer heard, seen, felt.

Numbness, hopelessness, bitterness, blink.

Accounts emptied, hunger pangs, souls lost.
Commence the maze of darkness.
Visions of graveyard games and lost bets fill the night.
Cheeks, salt-stained; eyes, glossy with complete disinterest.
Pain is no longer enough, strong, valid.

Numbness, hopelessness, bitterness, blink.

The positive diagnoses, loneliness suffocating, love absent.
Commence the maze of darkness.
Fading memories covered in junk food and careless lies.
Razors and mirrors pierce the mind into distraction.
Existence is no longer relevant, necessary, worthy.

Numbness, hopelessness, bitterness, blink.

DIFFERENT

Thick glasses among all the LASIK post-ops and daily contacts.
Late bloomers, insect collectors, banana flavors, and green skittles.
Lover of country music and old-school punk with matching neon hair.
Your lanky height, tattooed arms, and melanin-rich skin warrant stares.

Skipped classes and overdue bills merit Cs and cold nights,
But toothless giggles and baby's first words caress your exhausted heart.
Missed parties and meetings for the six o'clock train to relieve Grandma of babysitting duties.
Hunger pangs finally squashed by Mama's goulash; baby's all packed—forward, march!

Your portfolio is a mixture of recipes and play-date reminders,
Void of investment tips and Tinder hits.
Secondhand finds cover insecurities, never covered enough for invitations to the men's club,
A reminder of life's cruel, never-ending gym class, praying not to be picked last … again.

Your gay hips and liberal mind cause rumbles,
But the thoughts of world peace and inequalities pour out with ease.
Your difference changed a life, sparked a movement because you dared,
Dared to be a writer, a poet among scientists and surgeons,
Dared to be different.

DOUBT

The hesitating cat prowls back and forth before the jump.
The questioning student circles A then B then A again.
The lover fumbles his words before asking the man out.
The exhausted wife smells the cold leftover pasta before quickly eating at the sink.

The text from an unknown number.
The C on a paper well thought out.
The loans piling up for the newly carved career path.
The smell of another woman's perfume on his shirt.

A wavering color between yellow and red,
A reminder to reconsider before proceeding.
The sounds of smashing waves that rock the sailboat on cloudy days.
Your presence causes uncertainty, an evolutionary caution.

ENOUGH

Like still, blue sky reflecting ocean water,
Like calming wind atop beautiful hills,
Like the perfectly sugar-dusted doughnut,
You are peaceful.
You are enough.

Like the sight of a smiling, careless infant,
Like the stretching of a dreaming kitten,
Like the taste of a sweet summer blueberry,
You are simple.
You are enough.

Like the rough psoriasis-scarred triceps,
Like the anxiously overbitten lower lips,
Like the late nights, missed appointment, coffee breath,
You are worthy.
You are enough.

EXCITED

A child's itching to rip open presents on Christmas morning,
Screaming cousins reunited at last,
The wagging tail of a dog—
Excitement spreads through veins, leaving space for nothing else, perfumed joy.

Standing in front of a new home, freshly painted,
The front-row concert tickets with a lover,
The surprise eightieth birthday party for Grandma—
Excitement fills a room, leaving space for nothing else, loud laughter.

The acceptance letter to your dream school,
Riding down a snowy hill on a speeding sled,
The optimism of bright paths awaiting you—
Excitement blinds you, leaving space for nothing else, sailing high.

FEAR

The wide eyes with distorted lips,
Paralyzed by future shadows.
Your loud voice narrows the path,
An evolutionary advantage to keep heartbeats at bay.
Beneficial you are, at times.

The scattered brain with multiple options
Blanketed with doubt and hesitation.
Your broad shoulders hold me down;
Do not take the job, do not leap.
Limiting you are, at times.

The confused heart, reckless with passion,
Fluttering butterflies with calculated defenses.
Your frightening glares stifle my love.
Do not kiss the man, the woman, or else!
Irrational you are, at times.

27

FRUSTRATION

You taste like an over-sweetened, over-baked piece of forbidden carb.
You feel like endless confusing paperwork on a sunny day.
You look like the effortlessly chiseled abs of a 6-foot partygoer.
You hover like a solid C with an entire weekend used to study.
You push me to quit; your goal is to overpower my weaknesses.
You are a step ahead of anger.
But with a deep breath, your powers are harnessed, and you are drowned with true grit.

Your touch reminds me of the rolls of fat staring back at me minutes after my long run.
Your sounds are aggravating, exhausted grunts of curses.
Your desires constantly instructing my mind and body to give in, give up.
Your smell is of fresh seafood on a spring day, intriguing and nasty simultaneously.
You push me to quit; your goal is to overpower my weaknesses.
You are a step ahead of anger.
But with a deep breath, your powers are harnessed, and you are drowned with true grit.

The pain you cause is rarely necessary, calculatedly avoided, often overlived.
Your presence casts shadows of doubt and weights of exhaled sighs.
Your secret is that you can be avoided, or even more, repackaged and devoured to grow.
You push me to quit; your goal is to overpower my weaknesses.
You are a step ahead of anger.
But with a deep breath, your powers are harnessed, and you are drowned with true grit.

GRIT

The dried tears leave salt trails on your cheeks,
Doubt penetrates the mind, insecurities packaged in candy wrappers,
Routine smiles mask the layers of struggle and uncertainty
As grit tips the scale from contentment to perseverance.

The failures and rejections climb as hope dwindles;
Hours wasted; hundreds, thousands of dollars spent.
Giving up calls you in with open arms
As grit's sweaty, muscular face stares back at you,
Reminding you that success requires more hard work, more exhaustion.

Confusing skin color, ignorable stature, and emptied bank account,
Reminders of the outsider you are—classless, different.
Only grit's scream pushes you to get up, fight for your presence.
It will hurt, it will test you, it may break you.
But trust in grit to help you scrape your way over the finish line.

HAPPINESS

Happiness is the smell of fresh, gooey, chocolate chip cookies
That laid-back, deep exhalation, eyes-closed smile.
Happiness is that freshly cut summer grass and the cold morning mist on shoeless soles.
The taste of happiness jolts life.

Happiness knows no age; it guides the bones of your arthritic aunt on the dance floor.
It exudes its essence on windy nights as teenage lovers cuddle.
Happiness is sunsets on riverbanks with a book, with a boy, alone.
Happiness is that newborn infant curling up even more to the sounds of life.
The sight of happiness calms hearts and guides fireflies.

Happiness is that freshly dried, maroon-colored cotton blanket.
The touch of a lover's tongue as it caresses your ribs.
Happiness is the unwavering, overly wagging, cold nose, lick of a pup.
The touch of happiness ripens mangoes.

Happiness sometimes sounds like the enormously loud, deep belly laughter of your neighbor.
Or else happiness sounds like the puckered end of an innocent kiss from an old friend.
Happiness beats church bells and stills ocean breeze.
Happiness is the fully authentic giggle of a curious toddler.
The sound of happiness calms bustling waves and syncs Christmas carolers.

Happiness tastes like smothered smokey ribs;
It's the perfect amount of sweet and sour that you crave again.
Happiness is cabbage covered or panko fried or sugar glazed.
Happiness is a dirty martini with the right amount of joy.
The taste of happiness leaves us wanting more.

33

HOPE

When the barrel is empty and the sun dims, hope is all that is left.
It's easily overlooked and often unpolished, but it's there.
Some of us can use it easily, and others never sense its beauty.
Hope isn't trying to hide and doesn't want to be confused with desperation.
Hope is deep in the gut, hope is folded into your cells; like DNA, it wants to be read.

Hope sits, and hope waits; it knows you'll need it someday, maybe not today, maybe not tomorrow, but someday.
Hope paves the way, shining bright lights even when it's ignored.
Hope is often underestimated.
Hope is intangible, but hope can be harnessed and devoured to push through tough times.
Hope reminds you to keep pushing even when the weight of your burdens nearly suffocates you.
Hope begs to be used.

Hope is different and unique to each of us.
Hope is strong.
Hope is better than strong; hope is malleable and can be pounded into different shapes and pictures, peoples, and dreams.
Hope wants to remind you of its presence.
When all is stripped away, hope is the last thing left; its beaming face will be there.
Hope doesn't cost a thing; hope simply wishes you would say hi.
If you're lucky, you will respond, "Hi."

HOPELESS

The blank stare that absorbs no light,
The missing desire to care,
The gloomy sight of bare existence,
And the bland taste of repetition.
I wish I cared; no I don't.
I feel nothing; I am hopeless.

I float, I wander, my interest mostly gone.
I've been up, I've been down; today I'm numb.
One reason, or a million,
I wish I cared; no I don't.
I feel nothing; I am numb.

I've cheated, I've lied, my outlook sometimes gray.
My eyes constantly stare; I see nothing.
Her beauty should arouse my being, but it doesn't.
I wish I cared; no I don't.
I feel nothing; I am lost.

I live, I breathe, my head mostly down.
Bills are piling; job's just there.
Automated smile and robotic waves fill the day.
I wish I cared; no I don't.
I feel nothing; I am hopeless.

JEALOUSY

Jealousy is the hesitated half smile,
And the I-can-do-it-better attitude.
Life's reminder of human competitiveness.
Your shine can sometimes be outshined.
The growing self-doubt accompanied by others' success.
Jealousy is the reminder that you aren't always better.
You just think you are.

Jealousy is the taste of your own overly salted dish,
The excuses that allow your poor decorum,
The spacious and obligatory half-hearted hug and rolled eyes.
Jealousy is the reminder that you aren't always nicer.
You just think you are.

Jealousy is the spreading of infantile rumors and constant comparisons—
My boyfriend's muscles are bigger than yours.
Jealousy is the ugly side of your human nature, better trained than celebrated.
My girlfriend's bruises are better hidden than yours.
Jealousy is the reminder than you aren't always happier.
You just think you are.
You just want to be.
You are jealous.

LIKE

Like is the prerequisite to love—
The warmup stretches before a sweaty workout,
The tangy appetizer opening your palate for the main course,
The nervous laughter before the passionate sex ensues.

Like is the prerequisite to love—
The raw potatoes before the crunchy chips are bagged,
The necessary baby steps before the running begins;
The days, months, years before wants turn into needs.

Like is the prerequisite to love—
The loud laughter in your best friend's voice before lending a shoulder,
The late replies and missed calls before the hours and days of protective worrying,
The selfish self-centered goals turning into shared support and pure altruism.

Like is the prerequisite to love—
In case I don't say it enough, I like you.
One day, maybe, I will love you; only I will know.
Maybe, maybe not.

LONELINESS

Loneliness, present, always there; everyone else, gone.
Your sunken heart, lackluster soul, and saddened eyes glare at me.
You fluster my mind with idle thoughts and wasted nights.
You, loneliness, are my friend, alone, you.

Running from rainbow fears and bloody fields and reckless deals,
Your shadow follows me, our silhouettes intertwined.
You selfishly provoke my addictions and vice, dice, and even lies.
You, loneliness, are my friend, alone, you.

Strayed from any dreams, hope, the theatre smoke becomes my cloud.
You taste like pickle brine and cheap wine, and smell of swine.
Your morose objective is to make me satisfied in your filth.
You, loneliness, are my friend, alone, you.

LOVE

Love is sweet, necessary, deep.
Love is the taste of your mother's leftovers,
The smell of your grandfather's aftershave,
The two-teeth crooked smiles of a chunky niece.
Feel it: Love is family, friends, pets, lovers.

Love is a piercing ballad that raises hair,
The movie that pokes at your heart, tears choked.
Love is the dancing bodies, half naked.
Love is the documentary that gives you purpose.
Embrace it: Love shows up in odd places.

Love is safety, a shared story with close friends.
Love is believing in others, yourself.
Donated finances to the underserved, time to projects.
Love is genuine smiles and warm hearts.
Give it: Love gives hope, returns invaluably.

Love breaks you down.
Love is the reason you cry in the shower, worry.
Love is the reason you protect, fight, stand your ground.
But love is cuddles on a Tuesday afternoon.
Love is far more than intimacy, a reminder to live, live hard.
Make it: Love is the reason blood flows, air inhaled.

Be it; be in love
With yourself,
With your family,
With your surroundings, others, time,
With your lover.
Because love is always the solution, always.

LUCKY

Your home is rich in wisdom and equal parts laughter.
Family large, lovers passionate, feelings valued.
Your dinner table flourishes with rich colors and folklore storytelling.
Meals organically seasoned, beers cold, curiosity genuine.
Your skin is smooth and full of energy, sweet to the lick, unscented.
Showers relaxing, exercise rejuvenating, body constantly desired.

Your aura is visible and cinnamon-dusted, always appropriately inviting.
Smile gleaming, looks blessed, empathy unquestioned.
Your goals are allowed, encouraged, and pursued without doubt.
Acceptance letters plenty, finances covered, self-belief warranted.
Your friends are positive, helpful, and simply caring.
Parties invited, hugs comforting, memories unforgettable.

Hopefulness is ubiquitous, always present, and self-satisfying.
Outlook positive, path paved, inner-peace calming.
Dreams are naturally high, calculatedly risky, and wins are bountiful.
Motivated by self, compensated deservingly, competition in favor.
Life is easier than most, blessed, mostly cushioned along the way.
Life luckily lived, if ever lived at all.

RAGE

The forceful ripping of collection letters
Or the unmediated spitting of verbal daggers
Or the knuckle prints on an unsuspecting overly rouged face,
Rage is inconsiderate, untimely, sick.

The unwelcome barks and pronounced pain,
Or the vengeful swings of a dull blade
Or the melted beauty from undiluted acid,
Rage is unforgiving, unnecessary, burning.

The broken dishes and slammed phones,
Or the fractured bones and wounded psyche,
Wrecked cars, and fragile lovers—
The aftermath paints shocks of awoken, sunken hearts.
Rage begets rage, better ignored.

REGRET

The moment is gone, the event over, night falls.
Honeydew vengefully turning sour.
All that is left are incomplete memories and nausea,
And a deep gut-twisting pain: regret.

Questions fill the brain's frontal lobe,
Clouded in dark thoughts, showered in tears, flooded with fear.
Teeth clatter, bones rattle, but the brain is stuck on repeat,
Rendering, What if? What if? What if?

That party … that boy … that trigger …
That night … that woman … that drink …
That bad deal … that wrong turn … that day …
That wasted beautiful energy and veins of boiled blood.
I regret having ever met you, regret.

SELFISH

You lurk behind pleasant smiles and constant nods.
You are mysterious, and you taste like whatever the moment offers.
Your beauty entices my body until your needs are met.
You take my words, my friends, my innocence, and breath.
You selfish bitch.

Your scent is smokey and sweet, fueled by gluttony.
You raise your head when to gain, and lower your hands when to give.
You use others' energy with no intent to repay.
I only wish your colors were neon bright, so I could find you sooner.
You take my pride, my wallet, my gullibility, and time.
You selfish bitch.

You ruin friendships in single events
And end passionate nights filled with regret.
Your crass opinions silence rooms and questions intent.
You resemble insecurity but possess venom.
Your fangs often confused with canines until you strike.
You take my voice, my hope, my vulnerability, and joy.
You selfish bitch.

SEXY

Your lips, cherry red, raw, delicious.
Your lips, they whisper goodness from the heart.
You are sexy!
Your hips, bilaterally arched, bootylicious.
Your hips used to cradle unborn life, biologic.
You are sexy!
Your tits, perky and firm, smooth and warm.
Your tits, tired and over-suckled, sagged, lumps removed.
You are sexy!

Your hair, full of waves, perfectly dapper.
Your hair, thinned, glistening scalp, gray.
You are sexy!
Your pair, hanging, excited, charged, fun.
Your pair, wrinkled, slow, tugback, single, removed.
You are sexy!

Your eyes batting with temptation.
Your eyes exhausted.
You are sexy!
Your skin, elastic, rose-colored, genetically blessed, smooth, glowing, perfectly perspired.
Your skin, scarred with experience, varicose and wrinkled, overstretched.
You are sexy!
Your tears, rare, unexpected, necessary, there, joy filled.
Your tears, constant, remorse, regretful, pensive, lost, saddened.
You are sexy!

Your mind, filled with lustful thoughts, hormone overdose, desire, in-the-moment nights, and primal urges.
Your mind, tired, forgetful, preoccupied, selfless, chronically confused, and too often practical.
You are sexy!
Your partner is the only one.
Your partner is number 100.
You are sexy!

SHAME

You paralyze me like slow, activating venom.
I dwell on your superficial beauty.
I often fold into solemn shadows.
There I'm alone, temporarily relieved,
Covered by you, shame.

You're sweet, too sweet, so cavity-causing
That I do not dare tell anyone.
Your presence is unknown, random.
Some days missing, other days constant.

But your undeniable suffocation motivates me.
Some days you give me the will to run, run faster;
Think, think harder; love, love deeper.
With the brush of a word, almost any word,
My heart races at the mention of your whispers:
"Dumb, incompetent, fat, loser."

UGLY

It stares directly back at you.
You stand emotionless, and you see nothing but simple ugliness.
The thinning hair a blatant reminder of a ticking clock.
The exhaustion of bad luck pasted around your eyes in dark circles.
The crooked teeth and bad breath of despair, a touch of poverty and disease.
Simple ugliness.

You taste disgust when the naked reflection of a worn body waves at you.
Too many nights of overeating and even fewer days of content.
Fingernails dirty, anxiety-bitten, though sharp enough to scrape your excess skin.
Your stretch marks widen, wrinkles deepen, and pores full with last night's makeup.
Your swollen ankles and flat feet halt movement.
Simple ugliness.

In the crevices of your dark heart, ugliness works overtime to penetrate your brain.
You abuse your spouse, your family, yourself—simple ugliness.
Your hands create more marks on the souls of others.
You are small, like your limited thinking and refusal of necessary help.
You believe the lies; you accept ugliness.
Pure ugliness, simple ugliness.

UNFULFILLED

Your silhouette casts doubts on my mid-level career,
Your loud voice echoes my liberal arts degree is not enough!
Your harsh knuckles, a reminder to "Do more!"
My solid B, autocorrected as a C in your eyes, a constant reminder that it's no A.
My successes always questioned, "Will I ever be enough?"

Hours at the gym, strict diets, nothing to show.
Meditation and self-reflection labeled wasted time.
You spit my homemade tomato soup out; you've had better.
My growth always compared, never satisfied: Will I ever be content?

Briefcases and first-class tickets traded for husbands and snotty-nosed kids,
Half-written manuscripts covered in half-eaten turkey clubs.
Two-seater convertibles returned for off-white minivans.
Reflected in your mirror as a path most paved.
Because of you, I wonder, *Will I ever be fulfilled?*

61

UNLUCKY

Your house is just a place right now, temporary, unlike the emotional bruises and bitter memories.
Family broken, lovers quarreling, feelings numb.
Your dinner table is lonely; the takeout bloats you and a reminder of constant urgency.
Meals artificially seasoned, stories gossip, curiosity lacking.
Your skin is harsh, worn, and rank from constant perspiration of worry.
Showers rushed, exercise nonexistent, body readily ignored.

Your aura is sharp, electrocuting, basic, and rarely inviting.
Smile missing, looks unfortunate, empathy drowned.
Your goals are rejected, encouraged by few, and pursued rarely.
Your friends are reckless, superficial, and simply selfish.
Parties uninvited, hugs scoffed at, memories regrettable.

Hopefulness is bleak, rarely present, and always confusing.
Outlook negative, path not paved at all, inner-peace scrambling.
Dreams are painfully unreal, uncalculatedly risky, and loses are too common.
Motivated by bills; compensated rarely, competition not in favor.
Life is harder than most, unlucky, mostly scraping through.
Life lived unfortunately, lived unluckily.

VULNERABILITY

Often foolishly confused with weakness,
Vulnerability exposes your strengths, your creativity, yourself.
The lights shine only on you; your hard moment is here, take the step, brand the spotlight.
Singers, writers, poets, surgeons embrace your open arms
To await criticism or applause.

The cloak surrounds your body, electrifying and terrifying.
The outcome often joy or tears or sadness, but mostly fear.
At the right moment, vulnerability births your bubbling truths.
Breathe it in and allow space for its beauty.

Vulnerability is the sweetest of unknown fruits.
Covered in a hard shell, if not broken, you lose out on its juices.
Acceptance of its forceful nature brings pain, deep, internal cuts.
Masks and disguises cover your heart, fold your emotions.
But when penetrated, vulnerability reminds you, at the right time, of what
And often who really matters to you.

Be vulnerable.

WORTHLESSNESS

My body's purpose is to be used by one, two, maybe a hundred more.
My opinions are often wrong, better stifled.
My thoughts are rotten, scattered below scorn and pity.
My life matters to no one. I.am.worthless.

I smell like shame and disgust, my head often lowered.
Eyes constantly unfocused, my views are irrelevant.
My father's face and my mother's voice reinforce my voided existence.
To the world I add no value. I.am.worthless.

I always accept whatever little is given to me; I deserve only less.
Breaking natural laws of energy, always consuming, never providing,
The uselessness of my presence printed on my scarred skin.
I am reminded of this, constantly, in all dark moments.
I have no purpose; I *think* I.am.worthless.

Printed in the United States
by Baker & Taylor Publisher Services